Unique ACCESSORIES
You Can Make and Share

by Mari Bolte

illustrated by Paula Franco

CAPSTONE PRESS
a capstone imprint

Table of CONTENTS

Pack your bags for fun with the Sleepover Girls! Every Friday, Maren, Ashley, Delaney, and Willow get together for crafts, fashion, cooking, and, of course, girl talk! Read the books, get to know the girls, and dive in to this book of cool projects that are Sleepover Girl staples!

Wear glam glasses that match your style, and pair them with a camera strap made from a sassy scarf. Revamp your shoes with fabric, glitter, or beautiful boot cuffs. Then relax with some yoga and aromatherapy. Grab some glue, phone some friends, and start crafting with your very own Sleepover Girls.

MEET THE SLEEPOVER GIRLS!

Willow Marie Keys

Patient and kind, Willow is a wonderful confidante and friend. (Just ask her twin, Winston!) She is also a budding artist with creativity for miles. Willow's Bohemian style suits her flower child within.

Maren Melissa Taylor

Maren is what you'd call "personality-plus"—sassy, bursting with energy, and always ready with a sharp one-liner. You'll often catch Maren wearing a hoodie over a sports tee and jeans. An only child, Maren has adopted her friends as sisters.

Ashley Francesca Maggio

Ashley is the baby of a lively Italian family. This fashionista-turned-blogger is on top of every style trend via her blog, Magstar. Vivacious and mischievous, Ashley is rarely sighted without her beloved "purse puppy," Coco.

Delaney Ann Brand

Delaney's smart, motivated, and always on the go! You'll usually spot low-maintenance Delaney in a ponytail and jeans (and don't forget her special charm bracelet, with charms to symbolize her Sleepover Girl buddies.)

Picture Perfect

Friends are more precious than any gemstone, so why not put them front and center with this pendant necklace? Be sure to make some for your precious pals too!

WHAT YOU'LL NEED

clear glue

1-inch (2.5-centimeter) clear flat-back glass gems

small photograph

craft knife

industrial-strength glue

1-inch blank bezel pendant

ribbon

1 Squeeze a small amount of glue onto the back of a gem. Set the gem on the photograph and press firmly to squeeze out any air bubbles. Let dry completely.

2 Use the craft knife to cut around the gem.

3 Squeeze a small amount of industrial-strength glue onto the center of the bezel. Press the gem into the bezel.

4 Use the craft knife to remove any excess glue or paper. Then let glue dry completely.

5 Thread pendant on ribbon to make a necklace.

Shoe Love

Dress up any outfit with a pair of sparkling sandals. Give a new pair of shoes some extra shine, or just give new life to a pair of well-loved kicks.

WHAT YOU'LL NEED

decoupage glue and foam brush

glitter

old pair of clean, dry dress shoes

1 Pour some decoupage glue onto a paper plate. Mix with an equal amount of glitter.

2 Paint the glue and glitter mixture onto the heel and underside of the shoe.

3 Sprinkle more glitter onto the wet glue and glitter. Use your fingers to gently press the glitter into the glue. Let dry completely. Repeat, if desired.

4 Add a final coat of just decoupage glue. Let dry completely.

Scarf Strap

It's no surprise that Ashley's camera looks as good as she does. This simple project makes it easy to change up your style with the seasons.

WHAT YOU'LL NEED

tea bag

scrap leather

heavy-duty scissors

two split rings and hooks

super glue

scarf

needle and thread

1 Fold the leather in half. Trace the tea bag shape onto the leather. The short edge of the tea bag should be even with the fold line.

2 Cut out the leather piece and unfold with the shiny side facing down. Slide a split ring onto the leather.

3 Spread a small amount of super glue onto both sides of the leather. Sandwich one end of the scarf between the leather. Bunch the scarf if necessary to keep the edges of the scarf inside the leather.

4 Sew along all the cut edges of the leather. Reinforce by sewing from corner to corner to make an X shape.

5 Repeat steps 1-4 to finish the other side of the strap. Clip the strap onto the camera.

Glam Glasses

These sassy sunglasses would make the perfect Sleepover Girl accessory for their spring-break trip to Whidbey Island. Play around with different papers for lots of glam looks!

WHAT YOU'LL NEED

eyeglass kit or small screwdriver

scrapbook paper

sunglasses

satin decoupage glue and foam brush

dimensional decoupage glue

1 Use the screwdriver to remove the sunglasses' temples (the part that goes over your ear.) Set the lenses and screws aside.

2 Trace the temples onto the scrapbook paper. Cut out and trim, if necessary.

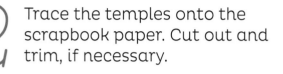

3 Brush a thin layer of satin decoupage glue onto the outside of the temples. Press the paper into the glue. Press out any creases or bubbles with your fingers. Let dry completely.

4 Place temples paper-side-up on a newspaper-lined work surface. Starting at one end, cover the scrapbook paper with dimensional glue. Use a rag to catch any glue drips. Let dry completely. Repeat with the other side of the temples.

5 Reattach the temples to the glasses' frame.

Fabric Flips

Show off your latest sleepover pedicure with these fun flip-flops. Bonus: fabric straps are comfier than the original plastic ones!

WHAT YOU'LL NEED

rubber sandals

scissors

four 4.5 by 24-inch (11.4 by 61-cm) pieces of fabric

super glue

⭐

1 Flip the sandals over. Cut off the rubber stoppers and remove the straps. Flip the sandals back over.

2 Cut the ends of the fabric pieces into points.

3 Stack one fabric piece on top of another Pull an end of the fabric through the sandal's toe hole. Tie the ends you pulled through into a double knot. Trim the excess fabric.

4 Flip the sandals over. Tie a looped knot about an inch from the top of the sandal.

5 Tie a second knot directly behind the first.

6 Separate the fabric and pull each piece through the side holes in the sandal. Figure out how tight you want the straps to be, and then knot the fabric into place. Trim the ends. Seal knots with super glue.

Relax Mat

Stretching before and after sleepovers is important! Breathe deeply and say, "Om ... "

WHAT YOU'LL NEED

polymer clay

soda or water bottle cap

stamp

toothpick

jump ring

cardstock

craft knife

masking or painter's tape

yoga mat

safety pin

essential oils

*

Oil Diffuser

1 Open the clay and knead with your hands until it's soft and pliable.

2 Pat or roll the clay out on your work surface until the clay is 1/8-inch (0.3-cm) thick.

3 Use the bottle cap like a cookie cutter to cut out circles.

4 Use the stamp to decorate the center of the circles.

5 Use the toothpick to make a hole near the top of each circle.

6 Set the clay circles on a baking sheet and bake according to the directions on the clay package. Let cool completely.

7 Thread a jump ring through the holes in the clay. Set aside.

8   Decide on a design and draw it onto the cardstock. Use the craft knife to cut out the design.

9   Tape the stencil to the yoga mat. Place the mat on a protected work surface before cutting out the design.

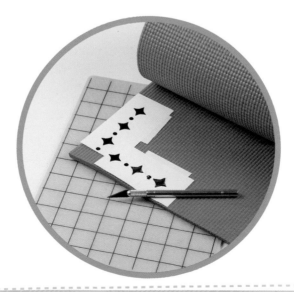

10 Decide where the clay circle will sit. Attach it to the mat with a safety pin.

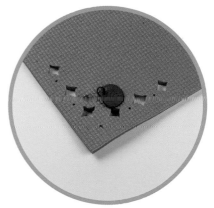

11 When ready to use, place a couple drops of essential oil on the clay circle.

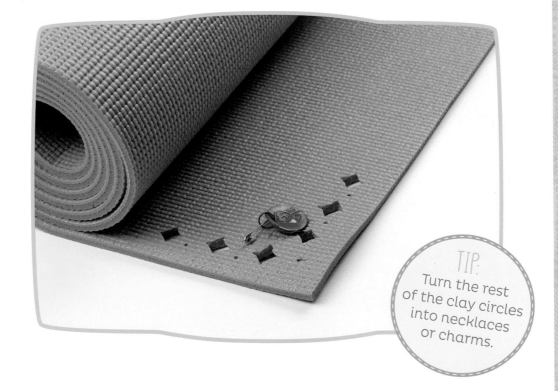

TIP:
Turn the rest of the clay circles into necklaces or charms.

Ribbons and Pearls

Maren likes to keep things simple and classic. Ribbons and pearls are the perfect accessory for both casual outfits and wedding-wear!

WHAT YOU'LL NEED

2-foot- (.6-meter-) long piece of .5 mm stretchable jewelry cord

collapsible eye needle

1 yard (0.9 m) piece of 3/8-inch (1-cm) satin ribbon

12–16 12mm glass pearls

liquid seam sealant

*

1 Thread the cord through the eye of the needle. Tie the ends of the cord together several times.

2 Tie a loose knot 6 to 7 inches (15.2 to 17.8 cm) from the end of the ribbon. Thread the jewelry cord through the knot. The needle end of the cord should come out the long side of the ribbon.

*

3 Tighten the knot around the end of the jewelry cord. For extra security, use the needle to make a few small stitches near the knot.

4 Thread a pearl onto the needle until it reaches the end of the cord.

5 Fold the ribbon over the pearl. The edges of the fold should be even with the side of the pearl. Sew in place.

6 Repeat steps 4 and 5 until the bracelet is the desired length. Then knot the cord to hold the last pearl in place.

7 Knot the jewelry cord and the ribbon together. Trim the end of the cord.

8 Trim the ends of the ribbon and seal the cuts with liquid seam sealant. To wear, tie the ribbon ends together in a knot or a bow.

Wilderness Bag

Be ready for anything with this well-stocked wilderness bag! Keep simple necessities nearby when you're on a hike or just away from home.

WHAT YOU'LL NEED

two 7 by 9 inch (17.8 by 23 cm) pieces of scrap fabric

duct tape

stapler

¼ inch (0.6 cm) hole punch

¼ inch eyelet setter

paracord

lighter

carabiner

1 Flip the fabric over so the bright side is face down. Cover the back of the fabric with strips of duct tape. Slightly overlap the strips.

2 Stack the two pieces of fabric together with the duct tape facing out. Staple the two short edges and one long edge.

3 Cover the staples with more duct tape.

4 Flip the bag right side out.

5 Punch two holes along the top of the bag. Repeat on the other side of the bag. Set an eyelet in each hole.

6 Loop paracord through the holes to keep the bag closed. Leave enough paracord at the end to loop around your wrist.

7 With an adult's help, use a lighter to melt the ends of the paracord to keep it from unraveling. Knot the paracord around the carabiner.

Pretty Ponytails

Delaney's simple style doesn't mean she doesn't need a way to hold back her hair!

WHAT YOU'LL NEED

ruler

scissors

3/8-inch (0.6 cm) foldover elastic

beads (optional)

lighter

2 by 6 inch (5 by 15.2 cm) card stock

stamps or stickers (optional)

1 Measure and cut a piece of elastic to 9 inches (23 cm) long.

Thread one or two
beads onto the elastic,
if desired.

Fold the elastic in half. Tie
a knot near the tail of the
elastic, leaving about a ½-inch
(1.3-cm) tail.

 Use the scissors to trim
the ends of the elastic
at an angle.

Have an adult use the lighter to
melt the ends of the elastic. This
will prevent the ends from fraying.
Repeat steps 1–5 to make as many
hair ties as desired.

 Slide 4 to 5 hair ties onto the
card stock. Decorate with
stamps or stickers, if desired.

TIP:
To make a
headband, use
elastic about
20 inches (51 cm)
long and follow the
same steps.

Boot Cuffs

Recycle an old sweater with these sweet boot cuffs. Change up the lace, sweater shades, and buttons for countless style options.

WHAT YOU'LL NEED

old sweater

lace trim

sewing pins

needle and thread

four small buttons

✻

1 Remove the arms from the sweater by cutting straight up from the armpit seam.

2 Pull the sleeve over your leg to stretch it.

3 Remove the sleeve and turn it inside out.

4 Pin the lace to the cut end of the sleeve about ¼ of an inch (0.6 cm) from the sleeve's edge. The decorative edge of the lace should face the down. Sew the lace in place. Remove the pins.

5 Turn the sleeve inside out. Fold the cut end of the sleeve over about ½ inch (1.3 cm) so the lace peeks over the top. Sew the fold in place.

6 Turn the sleeve right side out. Sew buttons near the top of the cuff.

7 Repeat steps 2–7 to make a second boot cuff.

Star-Powered Leggings

Everyone knows that Maren has star power, but these patterned leggings will let her show it. Try using glitter paint to really make them shine!

WHAT YOU'LL NEED

cardboard

newspaper

leggings

pencil and paper

foam sheets with sticky backs

foam brush

fabric paint

*

1 Trim cardboard so it fits inside the leggings. This will prevent paint from bleeding through the fabric. Line your work station with newspaper too.

* 2 Sketch your design onto a sheet of paper. Stick with simple shapes and patterns.

3 Trace and cut out the shapes onto the foam. Duplicate each shape so you have five of each. Peel the paper off the adhesive backing and stack the five shapes on top of each other.

4 Lay the papers across the leggings to use as guides while stamping, if desired.

5 Use a foam brush to apply paint to the non-sticky end of the stamp. Then stamp your pattern onto the front of the leggings. Set the leggings aside until the paint is dry enough to touch without coming off on your finger.

6 Flip the leggings over and stamp the back of the leggings. Let the paint dry and then wash as directed by the instructions on the label

No-Sew Apron

An old dress is transformed into a new apron with this no-sew project. It's just the thing Ashley needs to help her mom cook up some of that famous Maggio pasta!

WHAT YOU'LL NEED

old dress
scissors
iron
fusible tape
ribbon

✳

1 Lay the dress flat on your work surface. Cut along the side seams to separate the front of the dress from the back.

2 If your dress is not a tie-behind-the-neck style, cut off the old straps. Measure a piece of ribbon long enough to fit over your head. Then have an adult help you use fuseable tape and iron to attach the ribbon to the apron.

3 Fold in the sides of the apron to create a new seam. Iron the fold line so it's crisp. Fold over again and iron again.

4 Place fusible tape between the layers of folded fabric. Iron until the fusible tape melts. Repeat for the other side of the apron.

5 Measure and cut a piece of ribbon long enough to wrap around your waist. There should be enough left over to tie the ends in a bow.

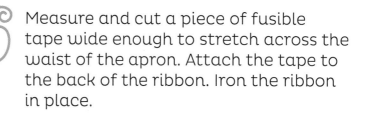

6 Measure and cut a piece of fusible tape wide enough to stretch across the waist of the apron. Attach the tape to the back of the ribbon. Iron the ribbon in place.

Read More

Berne, Emma Carlson. *Jewelry Tips and Tricks.* Style Secrets. Minneapolis: Lerner Publications Company, 2016.

Kuskowski, Alex. *Cool Refashioned Odds and Ends: Fun and Easy Fashion Projects.* Cool Refashion. Minneapolis: ABDO Publishing, 2016.

Turnbull, Stephanie. *Cool Stuff to Sew.* Cool Stuff. Mankato, Minn.: Smart Apple Media, 2015.

Snap Books are published by Capstone, 1710 Roe Crest Drive, North Mankato, Minnesota 56003.

www.capstonepub.com

Library of Congress Cataloging-in-Publication Data
Bolte, Mari.
  Unique accessories you can make and share /
By Mari Bolte.
    pages cm. — (Snap books. Sleepover girls crafts)
  Summary: "Step-by-step instructions, tips, and full-color photographs will help teens and tweens create fun accessories"—Provided by publisher.
  ISBN 978-1-62065-176-6 (library binding)
  ISBN 978-14914-6541-7 (eBook PDF)
1. Handicraft for girls—Juvenile literature.
2. Dress accessories—Juvenile literature. I. Title.

TT171.B655 2016
745.50835—dc23   2015023063

Designer: Tracy Davis McCabe
Craft Project Creators:
The Occasions Group
Creative Director: Nathan Gassman
Production Specialist: Laura Manthe

Photo Credits:
All photos by The Occasions Group
Photo Studio

Artistic Effects:
Shutterstock

Printed in the United States of America in North Mankato, Minnesota.
032015   008823CGF15